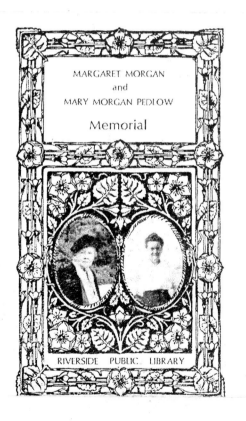

MARGARET MORGAN
and
MARY MORGAN PEDLOW

Memorial

RIVERSIDE PUBLIC LIBRARY

Andrew Jackson

Andrew Jackson

Kieran Doherty

AMERICA'S

7TH

PRESIDENT

Children's Press®
A Division of Scholastic Inc.
New York / Toronto / London / Auckland / Sydney
Mexico City / New Delhi / Hong Kong
Danbury, Connecticut

Library of Congress Cataloging-in-Publication Data

Doherty, Kieran.
    Andrew Jackson / by Kieran Doherty.
      p. cm. — (Encyclopedia of presidents)
    Summary: Discusses Andrew Jackson's childhood, family life, campaign-
ing, election, run for reelection, life after the presidency, and legacy.
Includes bibliographical references and index.
  ISBN 0-516-22760-2
   1. Jackson, Andrew, 1767–1845—Juvenile literature. 2. Presidents—United
States—Biography—Juvenile literature. [1. Jackson, Andrew, 1767–1845.
2. Presidents.] I. Title.II. Series.
E382.D64 2003
973.5'6'092—dc21   2002008271

CHILDREN'S PRESS and associated logos are trademarks and or registered
trademarks of Scholastic Library Publishing. SCHOLASTIC and associated
logos are trademarks and or registered trademarks of Scholastic Inc.
1 2 3 4 5 6 7 8 9 10 R 12 11 10 09 08 07 06 05 04 03

Contents

Chapter 1

The Most Roaring, Rollicking Fellow

"Give It to Them, My Boys"

A little after dawn on January 8, 1815, two signal rockets soared into the sky over a large field about ten miles (16 km) south of New Orleans. As the rockets hung in the sky, thousands of British soldiers in their scarlet coats set out across the field, marching in perfect order. A motley army of American farmers, militiamen, sharpshooters, and pirates waited. The Battle of New Orleans was under way.

As the British came within range, the Americans opened fire. Volley after volley of small arms and cannon shot smashed into the advancing redcoats. General Andrew Jackson, the American commander, shouted a command. "Give it to them, my boys," he called. "Let us finish this business today."

Andrew Jackson's men loved and trusted him. When he commanded, they obeyed. Cannon and small arms fire thundered. Scores, then hundreds of British soldiers and officers tumbled to the ground.

The Battle of New Orleans was the last major battle in the War of 1812 between the British and the United States. It lasted only about two hours. By the battle's end, more than 1,550 British soldiers lay dead or wounded. American losses amounted only to 13 killed, 39 wounded, and 19 missing.

The American victory over the British gave notice to the world that the young United States of America was a nation to be reckoned with. The victory also made Andrew Jackson a national hero and finally helped elect him the seventh president of the United States.

Birth and Boyhood

Andrew Jackson was born on March 15, 1767, in a log cabin in the Waxhaw region, on the border between North and South Carolina. His father, also named Andrew, and his mother, Elizabeth, were immigrants from northern Ireland who had come to the Carolinas only two years earlier. When they arrived, the Jacksons already had two sons, two-year-old Hugh, and Robert, a baby of six months.

Settling in the Waxhaw region, the elder Andrew Jackson cleared land, built a log home, and planted crops. He barely had time to reap a harvest, however, before he died in early March 1767. Elizabeth Jackson, who was expecting another child, took her two sons and moved in with her sister, Jane Crawford, a

A sketch of a modest cabin in the Waxhaws region where Andrew Jackson may have been born in 1767.

few miles away. Only days after she arrived, she gave birth to a baby boy. She named him Andrew in honor of her dead husband.

For the first twelve years of his life, Andrew lived in the Crawford home with his mother and two brothers. At the age of about six, he began school, where he learned reading, writing, and arithmetic, and, later, a smattering of Greek and Latin. His mother encouraged his studies, hoping that he would one day become a minister.

Instead, he seemed headed for trouble. He had a terrible temper. He was always ready to fight to get his way. When he was angry, he could curse a blue streak. When he was in a good mood, he loved to wrestle or race or tease or play

Where Was Andrew Jackson Born?

Both North and South Carolina claim Jackson as a native son. Some historians—North Carolinians themselves—believe Jackson's mother went to the home of a relative on the North Carolina side of the border and that Andrew Jackson was born there. Jackson, however, always claimed he was born in South Carolina.

Two high school football teams in the region settle the question every year. In the game between Union County (North Carolina) and Lancaster County (South Carolina), the winning team gets to claim Andrew Jackson as its native son for the following year.

☆☆☆

pranks. "No boy ever lived who liked fun better than he," said a boyhood friend. Then, about the time he turned 13, things got serious.

Jackson in the Revolution

Since 1775, the American colonies had been fighting Great Britain for their independence. In 1780, the war visited the Carolinas, turning the Waxhaw region into a bloody battleground. British soldiers and Americans loyal to Britain attacked the patriot militia, and the patriots fought back. After one of these skirmishes, in June 1780, Andrew's 16-year-old brother Hugh died of heatstroke. Soon afterward, 13-year-old Andrew and his brother Robert, then about 15 years old, went to serve in the militia themselves.

In 1781, the two boys were captured by a British unit. Soon, Andrew's sense of fairness got him into trouble. An English officer ordered Andrew to clean his boots. Andrew refused, replying angrily, "Sir, I am a prisoner of war, and claim to be treated as such."

Outraged, the officer struck at Andrew with his sword, slashing his hand and scalp. He then turned his anger on Robert, smashing him to the floor. The boys were sent to a crowded, filthy prison about 40 miles (60 km) from home. After

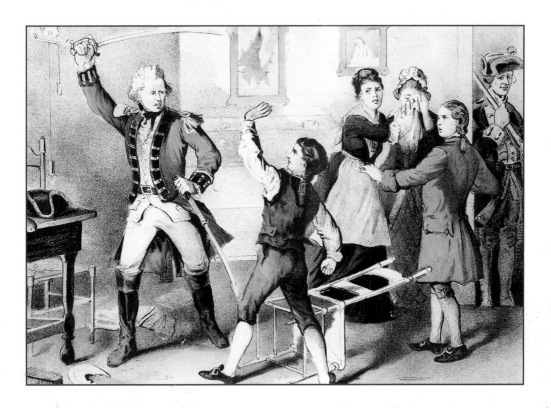

Held captive by British troops in the Revolutionary War as a boy of 13, Jackson refused to polish the boots of a British officer. The officer struck him with a sword, leaving a scar on his forehead that was visible the rest of his life.

ANDREW JACKSON

several months, they were freed in a prisoner exchange. By the time their mother arrived to bring them home, both had caught smallpox, a disease that often proved fatal. The mother and the desperately ill boys traveled homeward for two days. By the time they arrived, Andrew and Robert were barely alive. Robert died two days later. Andrew was desperately ill for weeks, but gradually, he recovered.

Soon afterward, Elizabeth Jackson traveled to Charleston, South Carolina, the colony's largest city, to care for prisoners. Soon after her arrival, she fell ill with cholera and died. Andrew Jackson, 14 years old, was left an orphan with no mother or father and no brothers. In addition, the blows of the British officer had scarred him for life. He was filled with hatred for the British, a hatred that would later make him a terrible enemy.

Training for the Law

After his mother's death, Andrew lived with relatives in the Waxhaw region. He found work making and repairing saddles and other gear for horses. He also had time to find trouble. A group of idle boys from Charleston had come to the Waxhaws to escape the British, who still occupied their hometown. Andrew spent his time with them, drinking, gambling, and staying out late. In December 1782, when his new friends returned to Charleston, 15-year-old Andrew Jackson followed them to the big city. There he continued his wild ways. Drinking and gambling, he quickly wasted a small inheritance he received from his grandfather. Broke, he returned home.

Back in the Waxhaw region, Andrew returned to school and finished his education. Rebellious as he was, he was a bright young man, and he learned quickly. Although he was bright, he never received a good education, even for his own time. In his letters, his grammar was shaky and his spelling was atrocious. He could spell the same word three or four different ways on a single page. He was smart enough to work for a brief time as a teacher at a local school, but he was not cut out to spend his days in the classroom.

In 1784, Andrew Jackson decided to become a lawyer. At the age of 17, he was as tall as a man. He was thin, as he would be throughout his life. His face was long and slender, almost gaunt, topped by a mane of sandy-colored hair that turned red as he grew older. According to those who knew him, Jackson's eyes were his most striking feature. They were bright blue, penetrating and alive with intelligence.

He said good-bye to the Waxhaw region and rode his horse 75 miles (120 km) north to Salisbury, the county seat of Rowan County, North Carolina. Soon after arriving in Salisbury, Jackson persuaded Spruce McCay, a well-known attorney, to let him study law in his office. For the next two years, he swept floors, copied legal papers by hand, ran errands and—when his other duties allowed— read law books and attended trials to see the law in action.

Not all Jackson's time in Salisbury was devoted to cleaning McCay's office and reading law books. He lived in one of the town's boardinghouses with several other student lawyers, including a young man named John McNairy. Jackson, McNairy, and several others formed a kind of club, dedicated to having a wild time. In those years, Jackson earned a reputation as "the most roaring, rollicking, game-cocking, horse-racing, card-playing, mischievous fellow that ever lived in Salisbury."

After about two years, Jackson, then aged 19, left McCay's office to study with Colonel John Stokes, one of North Carolina's most accomplished lawyers. Six months later, on September 26, 1787, following an examination by two judges, he was licensed as a lawyer. For the next six months, Jackson tried to get clients, but had little success.

In early 1788, his friend John McNairy was elected Superior Court judge for the western district of North Carolina, in the region that would soon become the state of Tennessee. In his role as judge, McNairy offered Jackson the job of public prosecutor for the district. Jackson quickly accepted McNairy's offer. A few weeks later, Jackson, McNairy, and several other friends headed west to seek their fortunes. Like the others, Jackson traveled on horseback, carrying a rifle, with all his belongings in a saddlebag.

Chapter 2

Nashville

When Andrew Jackson moved from North Carolina to the Tennessee region in the spring of 1788, he left the settled part of the United States for the dangerous frontier. Thousands of settlers from the east had pushed their way into the region, but it was so large that they were thinly settled. The settlers cleared fields and built houses on lands that belonged to the Cherokee and Creek, Native Americans who still lived in the region. Understandably, these native people fought to keep their land. They attacked settlements of whites and burned isolated farm cabins. One Native American leader described the area as "a bloody ground."

Jackson arrived in Nashville in October 1788. The town had been established only nine years earlier and was clustered around a series of small enclosed forts built on the bluffs overlooking the

Cumberland River. Cabins and other buildings were built close enough to the forts so that settlers could run inside at the first hint of danger.

Nashville offered some of the conveniences of civilization. It was home to several stores, two taverns, a whiskey distillery, and a school. Still, it was a frontier town located in an untamed region. Nashville and the surrounding area (soon called West Tennessee) included rough men who borrowed money and were not concerned about paying it back. As the prosecutor, Jackson had the job of going after these debtors and other lawbreakers. As he succeeded in bringing them to justice, he became popular with the region's law-abiding citizens. He still had time to practice law privately, helping people draw up deeds and wills and various business contracts.

Rachel Robards Jackson

Soon after arriving in Nashville, Jackson rented a room at the home of Mrs. John Donelson, the widow of one of Nashville's earliest settlers. Mrs. Donelson offered room and board to young men recently arrived in Nashville. There Jackson, then 21 years old, met Mrs. Donelson's daughter Rachel. The same age as Jackson, Rachel was a lively young woman with raven hair and dark brown eyes.

At the time, Rachel was married to Lewis Robards, but the marriage had been a disaster. Rachel had left the violent, jealous Robards and returned to

Nashville to live with her mother. Robards was living in Kentucky. During the next few years she made up with her husband, but then left him again and returned to Nashville a second time. When he threatened to come and find her there, she fled to Natchez, Mississippi, some 400 miles (650 km) to the south, where she stayed with friends. By this time, Andrew Jackson had fallen passionately in love with Rachel, and she with him.

In the summer of 1791, Jackson received information that Robards had divorced Rachel in Kentucky. He rushed to Natchez and told Rachel the good news. Soon afterward, they were married. It later turned out that Robards had filed for a divorce, but the divorce itself was not granted for more than two years. When the Jacksons learned of the error, they were married a second time in Nashville in January 1794. Years later, Jackson's political enemies would discover the facts about Rachel's divorce and her two weddings to Jackson. They would charge Rachel with *bigamy*—being married to two men at the same time—and call Andrew Jackson an adulterer.

Andrew and Rachel Jackson would have no children of their own, but they did adopt Mrs. Jackson's nephew. The boy took the name Andrew Jackson Jr. The Jacksons also served as guardians for several children who were left fatherless or orphaned. These children would be a great comfort to Rachel during long periods when her husband was away.

Rachel Robards Jackson

In the years following his marriage to Rachel, Jackson became one of Tennessee's most successful lawyers and one of the region's leading landowners. Eventually he bought a plantation about twelve miles (20 km) from town. This plantation would later become his residence, known as The Hermitage.

Jackson and Slavery

Like many in Tennessee in his time, Andrew Jackson owned slaves. At one point, he owned as many as 150—men, women, and children—who worked in the fields on Jackson's properties or in the big house at The Hermitage. Today, slavery

The Hermitage

In 1804, Andrew Jackson purchased the land that became his home for the rest of his life. At first, he and Rachel and other members of the family lived in a comfortable log farmhouse on the property. It was a two-story house with one room on the ground floor and three rooms upstairs. Eventually, he added a second, smaller log house about twenty feet from the big house to serve as a kitchen and as slave quarters. In 1819, he oversaw the construction of a stately brick house built in Federal style. During his presidency, he remodeled the house, adding a wide porch and soaring white columns along its front. This two-story mansion, with its elliptical staircase leading from a wide foyer to the second floor, became the centerpiece of the plantation known as The Hermitage. The Hermitage today is a museum visited by thousands of people each year.

☆★☆

seems cruel and inhuman, but it was an accepted part of Andrew Jackson's society. Like others, he simply accepted it as a part of life. By the time he retired from the presidency, an increasing number of Americans were questioning slavery. The most extreme of these, known as *abolitionists*, began demanding that slavery be ended—or abolished—throughout the country.

Indian Fighter

Jackson also accepted the prevailing idea that Indians—as Native Americans were known—were untrustworthy savages. He believed that the only way to keep the settlers of Tennessee safe was to force the Indians out of the region and to kill those who resisted.

The Native Americans of Tennessee, meanwhile, had come to hate and mistrust the white settlers. They frequently attacked settlers, brutally slaying even women and children. Jackson helped defend Nashville against Indian attacks. He went on raids to avenge Indian atrocities. He could be a terrible enemy to Indians he considered dangerous. One of the men who fought by his side described him as "bold, dashing, fearless, and mad upon his enemies" when he was in battle.

As Jackson gained local fame as an Indian fighter, he began to achieve recognition in the political world of Tennessee. In 1795, Tennessee's population passed 60,000 and the territory became eligible to become a state. Jackson was named a delegate to the Constitutional Convention. In June 1796, Tennessee was admitted as the 16th state in the Union. Jackson was elected the new state's first U.S. congressman. Six months later, after one of the state's U.S. senators was removed from office, Jackson was elected by the state legislature to fill the vacant seat. Just 30 years old at the time, Andrew Jackson was the youngest man in the Senate, and he represented the newest state.

Jackson soon learned that he hated being a senator. He disliked life in the big city of Philadelphia, then the nation's capital, and was overshadowed by the distinguished older men in the Senate. He missed his wife, and he was unable to manage his farms and businesses, which were falling deep into debt. On April 16, 1798, he resigned his seat and returned to Tennessee.

Judge Andrew Jackson

In 1798, soon after his return home, Jackson was named one of Tennessee's three superior court judges, a position he would hold for the next half-dozen years. According to tradition, Jackson was a good frontier judge. One of his earliest biographers said his decisions were "short, untechnical, unlearned, sometimes ungrammatical, and generally right."

In Jackson's mind, his job as a judge was to dispense justice, no matter what it took. In one famous case, a lawbreaker refused to come to court to stand trial for a brutal crime. Jackson had himself sworn in as a deputy so that he could personally arrest the lawbreaker. The criminal, drunk and armed, was holding a crowd at bay when Jackson walked up waving two pistols of his own.

"Now," Jackson roared, staring into the criminal's eyes, "surrender, you infernal villain, this very instant, or I'll blow you through."

The criminal stared at Jackson, then meekly dropped his guns and surrendered.

Later, the man was asked why he'd given up without a fight after refusing to surrender to a posse. "Why," he answered, "when [Jackson] came up, I looked him in the eye, and I saw shoot, and there wasn't shoot in nary other eye in the crowd; and so I says to myself, says I, hoss, it's about time to sing small, and so I did."

Jackson the Duelist ───────────────────

Jackson had never lost his willingness to fight when he believed his honor had been questioned. Whether the issue was a gambling debt or a petty insult, he insisted that his adversary back down or be willing to fight. His enemies learned that he was particularly sensitive to questions about Rachel and his marriage. To suggest any criticism of her was to risk Jackson's anger, and that anger could be deadly.

One man who felt Jackson's anger was John Sevier, a hero of the Revolutionary War and the former governor of Tennessee. In 1802, Jackson and Sevier competed for the position of major general of the Tennessee militia. Sevier, who had just finished his term as governor, wanted the post for himself. When he lost the election to Jackson, he was angry. Later, when he met Jackson on the street in Nashville, he attacked him verbally and then made the mistake of insulting Rachel.

"Great God!" Jackson bellowed, "Do you mention her sacred name?"

In an instant, the two men were shooting pistols at each other. Perhaps because they were so angry, their aim was terrible. An onlooker was slightly wounded, but neither Jackson nor Sevier was scratched. After this public gunfight, Jackson challenged Sevier to a *duel*—a formal fight between gentlemen to settle a dispute. Dueling was illegal in many states, but was still common on the western frontier. Eventually, friends of the two men intervened and the duel was never fought. Jackson, however, considered Sevier an enemy until the end of his days.

A few years later, in May 1806, Jackson took offense when a rich young man named Charles Dickinson insulted Rachel. According to legend, the trouble between the two men started over an unpaid gambling debt. In the heat of anger, Dickinson insulted Rachel. The two men continued to exchange insults, and later

An artist's conception of a duel. Jackson killed Nashville lawyer Charles Dickinson in a duel in 1806. Jackson himself was seriously wounded, and the bullet remained in his body the rest of his life.

Dickinson published a statement calling Jackson a "scoundrel," a "poltroon and a coward."

This was more than Jackson could stomach. He immediately challenged Dickinson, one of the best shots in Tennessee, to a duel. The two men met at dawn. Dickinson fired first. His bullet shattered two of Jackson's ribs and lodged in his chest, where it would stay for the rest of his life. Terribly injured, Jackson still took aim and fired back. The bullet struck Dickinson in the stomach, and he later died of his wound.

Jackson's duels earned him a reputation—at least in the eastern states—as a hotheaded frontiersman. This reputation would stand in his way when he sought promotion as a soldier, but it never caused him lasting harm. For every person who criticized his behavior, there was another who admired his sense of honor and his willingness to defend it.

The Burr Conspiracy

In 1806, Jackson got involved in a matter much more serious than a duel. It might have ruined his career forever and even led to his being branded a traitor.

Aaron Burr, a leading politician from New York State, was vice president under Thomas Jefferson in 1804. He challenged Alexander Hamilton, a political rival and personal enemy, to a duel. Burr's shot was true, and Hamilton died of his wounds. Although Burr was never charged with a crime in Hamilton's death, his political career was ruined.

Determined to regain power, Burr hatched a plan to use armed force to invade the Spanish territories of Florida along the Gulf of Mexico. Jackson believed that the plan was to add these Spanish territories to the United States and agreed to help. However, Burr told others that he hoped to make these territories into a separate country with himself as the ruler. Fortunately, Jackson soon learned the truth and dropped out of the plan. When President Jefferson learned about Burr's plot, he announced publicly that it was a *conspiracy* (a secret plot) against the United States. The plot soon fell apart.

Burr was charged with treason for his plotting. He was not convicted, but he never served again in a position of public trust. If Jackson had not dropped out of the plan, his fate almost certainly would have been the same.

Following his close call in the Burr Conspiracy, Andrew Jackson retired from public life for several years. He lived quietly on his farm with Rachel, their adopted son, and several foster children. He raised a stable of racehorses and grew to be one of Tennessee's richest farmers. He continued to serve as major general of the Tennessee militia. He drilled his men regularly, making sure they were ready to fight, and led them on several forays against local Indians. What he wanted, though, was an opportunity to test his skill against a real enemy. "In the event of a war I will lead them on, to victory and conquest," he said in November 1807.

In 1812 Jackson got his chance to lead his men into battle when the United States declared war with England. His service in the War of 1812 would make him the most famous man in America.

Chapter 3

Major General

The War of 1812—sometimes called "the forgotten war"—was declared by President James Madison on June 18, 1812. By that time, 45-year-old Andrew Jackson had been the head of Tennessee's militia for a decade. During those years, he had seen very little military action. Hungry for excitement and for a chance for fame, and motivated by hatred for the British, he immediately volunteered his services.

At first, government officials had little interest in Jackson's offer to command soldiers. Powerful men in Washington, D.C., were not willing to forget or forgive Jackson's involvement in the Burr Conspiracy. They were also troubled by his personal reputation as a hot-tempered man who would fight a duel almost at the drop of a hat. Eventually, however, he received a commission as a major

What: Also known as the Second War of Independence

When: 1812–1815

Who: The United States against Great Britain

Where: In the United States, Canada, and on the Atlantic Ocean

Why: Americans were angry that Britain was restricting U.S. shipping, seizing cargoes and sailors from U.S. ships, and encouraging Indians on the frontier to attack American settlements.

Outcome: The Treaty of Ghent (ratified in 1815) ended British impressment of American seamen and the existence of British forts south of the Great Lakes. It extended U.S. fishing rights in Canadian waters and settled issues about naval forces on the Great Lakes and commercial relations between the two countries.

general of the United States Volunteers. At the same time, he was ordered to lead an expedition from Nashville to New Orleans, Louisiana.

"Old Hickory"

On January 7, 1813, Jackson led an army of more than two thousand men out of Nashville. Most of his troops rode flatboats down the icy Cumberland and Ohio Rivers to the Mississippi, while the cavalry marched south through deep snow and bitterly cold weather. When they reached Natchez, Jackson received orders to disband his army and send his men home. Politicians working to end the war had decided the expedition was too dangerous.

Jackson's troops were exhausted from their long march. They were without supplies and far from home. Only Jackson's strong will held the army together. "It is . . . my duty," he wrote to his wife during the march home, "to act as a father to the sick and to the well and stay with them until I march them into Nashville."

Jackson gave up his horses to carry sick men and ordered his other officers to follow his lead. He marched along with his hungry, freezing men, keeping their spirits up. He took money from his own pocket to buy food and other supplies. At some point during the long march, Jackson's admiring followers began talking about how tough he was. As tough as hickory wood, some said. And finally someone called him "Old Hickory." The nickname stuck.

Jackson and his men reached Nashville in May 1813. Soon after his return, Old Hickory's temper once again got him into a scrape. What started as a political argument eventually escalated into a gunfight in the lobby of a Nashville hotel. In the shoot-out, Jackson was wounded in the arm and shoulder. He was carried to a room in the hotel, and only quick work by a physician kept him from bleeding to death. Even so, it was several long weeks before he recovered. And when he up and about again, he carried two bullets in his body. The bullet from his duel with Dickinson was still lodged in his chest. A second bullet from his latest fight was jammed against the bone of his left upper arm. The bullets would cause him pain and frequent sickness for the rest of his life.

Hit by a gunshot, Jackson was carried to the Nashville Inn, where he was treated and stayed for several weeks while recovering.

War with the Creeks ————————————

In August 1813, Jackson was still recovering from his latest brush with death. News arrived in Nashville that a group of Creek Indians had attacked the Fort Mims settlement in present-day Alabama. The brutal attack killed about 250 men, women, and children.

News of the attack filled residents of Tennessee with terror. The governor of Tennessee quickly called for an army of volunteers and ordered Jackson to take command. Old Hickory rose from his bed weak and shaky, with his left arm in a sling, but strong enough to go to war. In early October, he was at the head of a small army marching into Alabama.

The campaign against the Creek was a miserable affair in every sense. Jackson and his men were thirsty for blood. As they entered Creek territory they savagely attacked and burned villages. In their desire to avenge the Fort Mims attack, they slaughtered as many Native Americans as they could. After a battle at one village, one of Jackson's soldiers bragged, "We shot them like dogs."

Even as they killed Indians, Jackson's troops were tormented by a lack of food and other supplies. At one point, they even threatened mutiny. Jackson responded with harsh discipline, ordering the execution of several soldiers, including an 18-year-old private who disobeyed an officer.

In March 1814, Jackson's men attacked a Creek settlement nestled in a bend of the Tallapoosa River in present-day Alabama near the Georgia border. The Creek had built a barricade across the neck of the bend so that their settlement was protected from attack by the river on three sides and by the barricade on the fourth. Jackson ordered a direct assault on the barricade.

About a thousand Creek fighters inside the barricade fought heroically, but finally were driven back by the Americans, who had a force at least twice as large. Of the Creek who fought, only 150 survived. The engagement, known as the Battle of Horseshoe Bend, ended the power of the Creek nation in Alabama and Georgia. That summer, Jackson negotiated the Treaty of Fort Jackson, forcing the tribe to give up about 30,000 square miles (78,000 sq km) of their lands.

Lyncoya

Following one of the battles against the Creek, a ten-month-old infant boy was found on the battlefield, clutched in the arms of his dead mother. When told of the baby, Jackson had him brought to his tent. Later the boy, named Lyncoya, was sent to The Hermitage, where he became Jackson's ward. He was raised at The Hermitage and treated like a member of Jackson's family. He died at the age of 16, probably of tuberculosis.

★ ★ ★

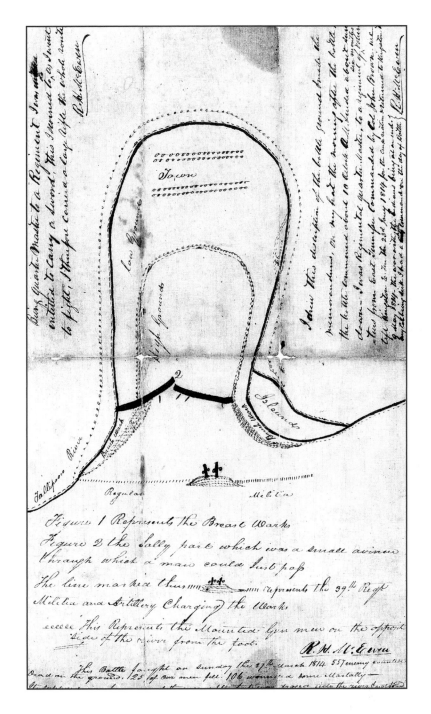

This map of Horseshoe Bend was sketched by one of the participants in the battle there. Jackson's men attacked the barricade at the narrowest part of the bend and overcame the Creek defenders after a hard fight.

Jackson receives the surrender of a Creek chief at Horseshoe Bend.

This victory was the first in Jackson's military career, and it made him a hero in the United States. At the end of the campaign, however, Jackson returned home exhausted and ill. He was partially blind, suffered from chronic lung problems, and had terrible headaches.

New Orleans

As Jackson recovered at The Hermitage, the War of 1812 was not going well for the Americans. In August 1814, the British captured Washington, D.C., and burned the Capitol and the White House. American forces soon rebounded with victories in Baltimore and New York State, but the British still controlled the seas. Late in the year, American military leaders learned that a British expedition was on its way to New Orleans, at the mouth of the Mississippi River. Many southern and western farmers floated their cash crops down the river and sold them in New Orleans. If the British captured the port, they would cut off American trade there.

Fresh from his victories over the Creek, Jackson was promoted to major general of the regular army, given command of the army in the southern United States, and ordered to head south to New Orleans.

Jackson organized a mixed group of regular army, militia, and volunteers. In New Orleans itself, he gained the support of nearly all elements of the population—French, Creole, Irish, and even free African Americans. He also gained the support of the notorious pirate leader Jean Lafitte, whose center of operations was nearby.

In December 1814 the British landed troops south of New Orleans. Jackson attacked their camp, but was unable to hold it. He retreated up the east

Jean Lafitte

Born around 1780, Jean Lafitte was the leader of a band of privateers and smugglers. In about 1810, he and his men set up headquarters in the area of Barataria Bay, near New Orleans. From there, they attacked ships in the Gulf of Mexico and stole their cargo. In 1814 the British attempted to buy Lafitte's aid in attacking New Orleans, but Lafitte offered his services to the Americans. At first, Andrew Jackson refused his offer, but he and Lafitte finally came to an agreement. Lafitte's pirates provided desperately needed naval support for the city's defense. After the battle, Lafitte returned to his life as a privateer. He died in about 1826.

Jean Lafitte, a notorious pirate who lived in New Orleans, provided naval support for Jackson's army at New Orleans.

side of the Mississippi toward New Orleans. At a narrow place between the river and an impassable swamp, he ordered his troops to construct a wall of cotton bales and mud. From there his expert marksmen could pick off red-coated British soldiers like ducks in a shooting gallery.

After two unsuccessful attacks on the Americans, the British made their major assault on January 8, 1815. Led by Sir Edward Pakenham, they advanced against the American earthworks in orderly columns. Each wave of attackers was cut down by the American defenders. Pakenham was killed and 2,000 British fighters were killed, wounded, or missing. An army from the world's greatest military power was almost destroyed by a ragtag bunch of Americans led by a sick, tired general with no formal military training.

It is one of the ironies of history that this terrible battle was fought for nothing. A treaty of peace ending the war had been signed in Europe on December 24, 1814, more than two weeks before the battle. News of the treaty did not reach New Orleans until weeks after the battle was fought.

Still, Americans rejoiced at the victory in New Orleans. It seemed to say that the threat of British interference in Amercan affairs had ended forever. Andrew Jackson became the most admired man in the nation, every bit as famous as a rock star or movie star today. Immediately, there was talk of electing him president of the United States.

An artist's conception of the Battle of New Orleans. U.S. troops held their lines against repeated attacks by the British. Jackson is at the right on the white horse.

That would have to wait, though, for Jackson was not yet through adventuring.

Florida

With the War of 1812 ended, Jackson marched once again into battle in 1818 against Native Americans. Seminole warriors were raiding settlements in southern Georgia and retreating into Florida, then a territory of Spain. On orders from the government in Washington, Jackson drove the Seminole out of Georgia and pursued them into Florida. Then, without orders, he captured the Spanish fort at St. Marks. He captured two British citizens. Claiming that they had helped the Seminole, he executed them.

Still, Jackson was not satisfied. He captured the Spanish fort at Pensacola, arrested the Spanish governor, and sent him with a shipload of Spanish officials and soldiers to Havana, Cuba. Then he returned to Georgia and traveled back to Nashville.

American settlers in Georgia—and many other Americans—cheered Jackson's exploits. The reaction in the nation's capital, however, was quite different. The United States was at peace with both Spain and Britain, yet a U.S. army had invaded the territory of one country and executed citizens of the other.

Jackson's men capture two Seminole chiefs in Florida during the Seminole War in 1817.

President Monroe and members of Congress were outraged at Old Hickory's high-handed tactics. Many in Monroe's cabinet urged that Jackson be *censured* (condemned officially) for exceeding his orders.

Only John Quincy Adams, then secretary of state, advised against censure, and he finally gained President Monroe's agreement. Adams used the incident to persuade Spain that it could no longer control Florida. Over the next two years, he persuaded Spain to sell Florida to the United States.

In the summer of 1821, President Monroe appointed Andrew Jackson the first governor of the Florida Territory. Jackson presided over the official transfer of the territory to the United States, but he did not stay long. Florida's hot, humid climate did not agree with him, and Rachel, who joined him in Florida, hated being away from The Hermitage.

When he resigned from the governorship in November 1821, Jackson was 54 years old. He was turning away from military command and toward political leadership. As always, Jackson aimed high—at the presidency of the United States.

Chapter 4

Angling for the Presidency —————

When Andrew Jackson arrived back at The Hermitage in 1821, he was in terrible health. The bullet lodged in his chest caused bleeding into his lung, and he coughed up blood almost constantly. The bullet in his arm pained him. He had frequent fevers and bouts of diarrhea.

At The Hermitage, he rested and regained his strength. He enjoyed the company of Rachel and his family, including children for whom he was the legal guardian. He also corresponded with friends across the country. One of his favorite topics was what he viewed as the "corrupt" state of the government. He was particularly angered by government officials who used their public offices for private gain.

Old Hickory's friends soon began talking about making him president of the United States. In July 1822, more than two years before the next election, the state legislature of Tennessee nominated him for the presidency. In October 1823, hoping to keep Jackson in the public eye, the Tennessee legislature elected him U.S. senator for the second time. (Before 1913, U.S. senators were elected by state legislatures, not by popular vote.)

During the next year, Jackson remained out of the spotlight while his backers worked to gather support for his candidacy. Like other men seeking the presidency in those days, he believed it was not proper for a candidate to campaign for himself. "The Presidential chair is a situation which ought not to be sought for . . .," Jackson wrote in a letter to a friend. Still, as the most popular

Political Parties in 1824

In 1824, there was only one major political party in the United States. The Democratic-Republicans had elected every president for 24 years—Jefferson, Madison, and Monroe, each for two terms.

The Democratic-Republican party was divided, however. On one side were conservatives like John Quincy Adams and Henry Clay. They supported government spending for improvements, such as roads and canals, and high *tariffs* (taxes on goods imported into the country) to encourage American manufacture and trade. They eventually became known as National Republicans. On the other side were more traditional Democratic-Republicans, who believed in a limited central government and spoke especially for small farmers and landowners. This wing of the party embraced Andrew Jackson.

☆☆☆

figure in the United States, Jackson gained wide support. With his approval, his backers promised that he would reform the corrupt government in Washington and return it to the control of the people.

The Election of 1824

The election of 1824 was a contest for control of the Democratic-Republican party. All four candidates claimed to have its interests at heart. Jackson was most popular among voters, especially in the fast-growing regions west of the Appalachian Mountains. William H. Crawford of Georgia had strong support in Congress and in the southern states. Both were traditional Democratic-Republicans. Running against them were two leaders of the new National Republican faction. John Quincy Adams of Massachusetts was the son of the second president and had served for eight years as the secretary of state to President Monroe. His greatest support was in New England. Finally, Henry Clay of Kentucky was the most powerful man in the U.S. Congress and a strong supporter of National Republican ideas.

Jackson was the outsider. Although he had served briefly in the House and the Senate, he had spent little time in Washington, D.C., and was known as a strong critic of the present government. He came not from Massachusetts or Virginia (the home of every president up to that day), but from the frontier of

Tennessee. His reputation as a fierce warrior with a hot temper worried many political leaders. What would happen if a backwoodsman like Jackson should become president? they asked. Still, no other candidate could match his accomplishments in battle or his engaging personality.

The right to vote for president in 1824 was still the privilege of a few. Only men who owned a certain amount of property could cast a ballot. This eliminated many of Jackson's strongest supporters. Even so, he proved to be the strongest vote-getter. He received 153,000 votes. John Quincy Adams received 116,000. Crawford and Clay received fewer than 50,000 each. In the electoral college, where the final vote is held, Jackson gained 99 votes, Adams 84, Crawford 41, and Clay 37. Since no candidate received a majority of the votes (half of the vote plus one), the final choice was left to the House of Representatives.

In February 1825, the House met to elect the new president. Jackson's supporters urged members of the House to vote for their man, who had gained the largest popular vote and the largest vote in the electoral college. Jackson's opponents, however, searched for a way to defeat him. Henry Clay, who finished fourth in electoral votes, was eliminated, but he held the balance of power. He urged House members whose states had voted for him to throw their support to John Quincy Adams.

According to the rules, each state delegation had one vote which it could cast for one of the top three candidates—Jackson, Adams, or Crawford. The winner needed to receive the vote of a majority of states, at least 13 of the 24. When the final vote was announced, John Quincy Adams had 13, Jackson 7, and Crawford 4. Adams was the new president.

A few days later, Adams nominated Henry Clay to serve as his secretary of state. When Jackson heard of the appointment, he was enraged. He and his supporters claimed that Clay and Adams had made a "corrupt bargain"—Clay's support in the presidential vote in return for his appointment as secretary of state. Adams and Clay denied that such a bargain had been made, but hundreds of thousands of Jackson supporters believed otherwise. Jackson had been elected by the people, they said, and the professional politicians had stolen the election from him.

In 1825, Jackson's supporters organized with two objects in mind. The first was to block any program proposed by the Adams administration in Congress. The second was to win the next presidential election in 1828. One of the main organizers of the Jackson program was Martin Van Buren, a U.S. senator from New York. Van Buren, famous for his skills as a political operator, had supported Crawford in the 1824 election. Soon after the election, he moved into Jackson's camp. In the next election, he was determined to back a winner.

When the House of Representatives decided the 1824 presidential election, Henry Clay (above) threw his support to John Quincy Adams (right), and Adams was elected. Clay became Adams's secretary of state. Jackson believed they had stolen the presidency from him.

The Election of 1828 ———————————————

In 1828, John Quincy Adams ran for reelection against only one major competitor, Andrew Jackson. The campaign was, by all accounts, one of the dirtiest in American history. Adams's backers painted a picture of Jackson as a violent man. They attacked him as a murderer for executing mutinous soldiers during the war against the Creek Indians. They called his mother a prostitute. They attacked Rachel Jackson as a bigamist and Jackson as an adulterer because they had married before her divorce was final.

Jackson's followers answered in kind. They attacked Adams for the "corrupt bargain" he had made with Clay in 1824. They portrayed Adams as un-American because he had lived for years in Europe as a diplomat serving the United States. They said he was an aristocrat who wasn't interested in the common people. They even condemned him for using federal funds to buy gambling equipment—a pool table for the White House.

There was never much doubt about the outcome of the election. Adams was a brilliant man but had never been a popular politician. The carefully organized Jackson campaign and Jackson's larger-than-life personality put President Adams in the shade. Voters saw Old Hickory as a man of the people and the hero of New Orleans. They agreed that it was time to change the government in

Andrew Jackson at about the time he was elected president in 1828.

Emily Donelson, a niece of Rachel Jackson, served in her place as White House hostess during Jackson's years as president.

Washington. Jackson gained nearly 690,000 votes, four times his total in 1824. Adams gained nearly 510,000. In the electoral college, Jackson had 178 votes to 83 for Adams. This time he had a clear majority.

For Jackson, the victory at the polls was soon overtaken by personal grief. Rachel had fallen into a deep depression over the ugly accusations made by Jackson's political enemies. On December 18, 1828, while preparing to move to Washington, Rachel suffered a heart attack. On December 22, she died. She was buried on the grounds of The Hermitage, in a corner of her garden.

In Jackson's mind, Rachel was a victim of the campaign of 1828 as surely as if she'd been murdered by his political enemies. He grieved his wife's death to the end of his days, and never forgave his enemies for what he described as "a loss so great" that it could "be compensated by no earthly gift."

Inauguration

On March 4, 1829, Andrew Jackson looked every inch a soldier as he walked to the Capitol for his inauguration as the seventh president of the United States. At the age of 61, he was forced to use a cane, but he still stood ramrod straight. Only Jackson's wrinkled, worn face showed his age, the ravages of his illnesses, and the grief he felt over the death of Rachel.

Jackson addresses supporters during his trip from Tennessee to Washington to take office as president in 1829.

After his swearing in, Jackson, dressed in a plain black suit, made one of the shortest inaugural speeches in history. He promised a benign presidency. "I shall keep steadily in view the limitations as well as the extent of the executive power," he said. He also promised to preserve states' rights, defend the Constitution, and preserve the Union.

A Mad, Wild Party

Following his inauguration, Jackson hosted a reception at the White House. Instead of inviting selected important people, he had a "people's party," throwing open the doors of the White House to everyone. Thousands of people swarmed into the mansion during the afternoon. They eagerly devoured cakes and ice cream and drank alcoholic orange punch. They tore the White House draperies, broke china, and almost trampled the new president. Longtime government officials were horrified at the disorderly party, but it added to Jackson's reputation as a president of all the people.

Within days, Jackson set about changing the federal government. He refused to reappoint officials who had held their jobs through previous administrations and viewed their offices as their own personal property. In their place, he appointed his supporters, opening many government positions to people who

Thousands came to Jackson's "people's party" on inauguration day. This drawing shows the crowds outside the White House.

had not studied at the best colleges and were not members of the most prominent families.

Jackson's enemies complained that he appointed loyal supporters even when they were not the best men for the job. He followed the lead of his campaign manager, Martin Van Buren, who had built a powerful political "machine" in New York by rewarding loyal party members with jobs and government contracts. This was known as the "spoils" system because one of Van Buren's men once said that in politics as in war, "to the victor belongs the spoils."

most dear," he said, suggesting that liberty was even more important than pre-serving the Union.

From that point on, the two men barely spoke.

The "Petticoat War" ————————————————————

Calhoun and Jackson finally broke relations altogether—not on a political issue, but on the issue of a cabinet member's wife. The newspapers called this episode the "Petticoat War."

At the beginning of his administration, Jackson appointed John Eaton, a former senator from Tennessee and a close friend, as secretary of war. Eaton, whose first wife had died, had recently married a lively, attractive woman named Peggy O'Neill, the daughter of a Washington innkeeper. Her first husband had committed suicide in 1828, and Washington gossip suggested that he was despon-dent because his wife was seen with other men.

Led by the wife of Vice President Calhoun, the wives of Jackson's cabinet members announced that they would not associate with Peggy Eaton. If she was invited to a reception or dinner, they would not attend.

The situation must have reminded Jackson of Rachel, who had been a tar-get of ugly gossip. He publicly defended Peggy Eaton, and angrily refused demands that he remove John Eaton from the cabinet. Jackson and Secretary of

Peggy O'Neill Eaton, wife of Secretary of War John Eaton, was shunned by other cabinet wives, causing a government crisis in 1831.

State Martin Van Buren came to social affairs with the Eatons even when the rest of the cabinet members stayed away. Jackson began meeting less frequently with his cabinet. Instead, he discussed important affairs with a group of trusted advisers that newspapers came to call his "kitchen cabinet."

Soon Jackson was no longer on speaking terms with his vice president or with three of his cabinet members. However amusing the "Petticoat War" might be, it was having serious consequences.

Finally, in 1831, Martin Van Buren settled on a plan to end the war. With Jackson's approval, Van Buren announced that he and John Eaton would resign from their cabinet positions to protest the conduct of the other members toward John and Peggy Eaton. Soon afterward, Jackson requested the resignations of all other members of the cabinet so that he could reorganize it. Some may have expected their resignations to be refused, but Jackson accepted them all. Then he appointed new cabinet members more likely to support his policies.

Nullification

In late 1832, Congress passed a new tariff act that did little to ease the burden on southern states. South Carolina's state legislature voted to nullify the tariffs of 1828 and 1832. The nullification acts authorized the state to stop collecting the federal tariff at ports in South Carolina. Soon afterward, Vice President Calhoun

South Carolina officials took over the federal customhouse in Charleston and refused to collect federal tariffs in 1833. Jackson threatened to use force to regain federal control, but the crisis was avoided by a compromise.

resigned and was appointed to the U.S. Senate, where he could organize support

for nullification.

Jackson issued a stern statement declaring nullification illegal and warn-

ing South Carolina that its actions might lead to war. He ordered the U.S. Navy to send ships to Charleston, South Carolina's harbor, with orders to fire upon the rebels if necessary. At the same time, however, he made it clear he was willing to compromise to avoid war and bloodshed. Moderates in South Carolina responded with signals that they, too, were willing to compromise.

The compromise was negotiated and sponsored by Jackson's old enemy Henry Clay. In March 1833, days before Andrew Jackson's second term began, Congress passed a new tariff act that gradually reduced tariffs over the next ten years. The combination of Jackson's threats and Clay's skill in negotiating brought an end to the crisis.

Removing the Bullet

In 1831, as Andrew Jackson battled the nullifiers, the bullet he carried in his left arm started to bother him. By that time it had moved so that it was near the surface of his skin. It hurt so badly that it began to disturb his work schedule. In early 1832, a surgeon came to the White House to remove the bullet. Doctors still had no effective painkilling medications, so Jackson simply grabbed his walking stick and said, "Go ahead." The surgeon made an incision, squeezed Jackson's arm, and out popped the bullet. Jackson, showing the strength that gained him the name Old Hickory, went right back to work.

☆☆☆

The compromise tariff bill of 1833 that helped end the crisis in South Carolina was worked out by two of Jackson's political opponents, Henry Clay (left) and John C. Calhoun (right).

The Monster Bank

At the same time that Jackson waged war on the forces of nullification, he went to war on another front. His enemy in this war was the Bank of the United States. The first Bank of the United States had been established in 1791 by Secretary of the Treasury Alexander Hamilton. Hamilton believed that the bank was important to the country to help manage the supply of currency (money) so that business among the states and with other countries would go smoothly. It was set up as a private corporation run by bankers who were not elected or appointed by the government. The federal government owned a small part of the bank's stock, and it agreed to use the bank for its own transactions. This made the bank the most powerful economic institution in the country.

When the first bank's *charter* (license to operate) expired in 1811, Congress refused to extend it, and the bank went out of business. Five years later, in 1816, Congress agreed to establish a second Bank of the United States, hoping that it could help solve financial problems caused by the War of 1812. The second bank was chartered for 20 years.

The Bank of the United States had many enemies. They claimed it was dangerous to the interests of common men and women, especially farmers and other rural people in the south and west. Because it was a private corporation, it was not responsible to the people or to lawmakers. Small farmers and tradesmen

The States During the Presidency of Andrew Jackson

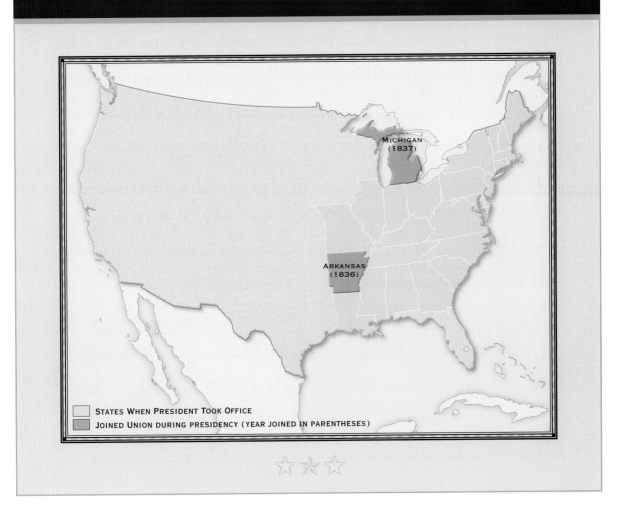

MICHIGAN
(1837)

ARKANSAS
(1836)

☐ STATES WHEN PRESIDENT TOOK OFFICE
■ JOINED UNION DURING PRESIDENCY (YEAR JOINED IN PARENTHESES)

☆ ☆ ☆

who needed loans resented the bank's power to set high interest rates. Settlers and land speculators along the western frontier believed the bank was run to protect eastern businesses and foreign investors.

The opponents of the bank found their champion in Andrew Jackson. He attacked the bank as a "monster" monopoly that benefited the rich and powerful at the expense of working men and women. He also disliked it because it was backed by some of his political enemies, financially powerful men who were opposed to his policies.

Near the end of Jackson's first term in office, his political opponents were looking for an issue that might defeat him in his campaign for reelection. The bank's charter still had four years to run, but they thought they could put him in a difficult spot if they brought the charter up for renewal during the campaign. If he approved a new charter, he would lose many of his supporters. If he *vetoed* it (refused to approve it), they could accuse him of ignoring the will of Congress and paint a frightening picture of him as a dictator. On July 3, 1832, only four months before the election, Congress voted to renew the bank's charter and sent the bill to the White House for Jackson's signature.

Jackson did more than simply veto the bank legislation. He issued one of the strongest veto messages ever issued by a president. In the past, presidents had vetoed bills of Congress only because they appeared to be unconstitutional.

Jackson vetoed the bank charter claiming simply that it was harmful to the country. He then dug in to fight the bank's supporters just as he had dug in to fight the British outside New Orleans. The Congress had the right to *override* Jackson's veto, but to do so, it needed to pass the bank bill in both houses by two-thirds majorities. Supporters of the bank could not find the votes to override Jackson's veto.

The Campaign of 1832 ———————————

During Jackson's first term of office, his supporters organized as never before. They enlisted the support of newspapers around the country and organized clubs in nearly every town and city. As the election of 1836 approached, they were prepared. In the past two elections, all the candidates were supposedly from the same party. Now the Jackson supporters announced the formation of a new party of the people, to be called the Democratic party. The party has gone through many changes over the years, but it continues to this day.

The National Republicans, the party of John Quincy Adams, nominated Jackson's old foe Henry Clay. At first, the National Republicans believed they had a chance to defeat Jackson. Clay, a strong supporter of the Bank of the United States, made it a major issue in the campaign. He attacked Jackson's veto as the act of a tyrant.

Martin Van Buren, Jackson's secretary of state and later his vice president, was the main organizer of the new Democratic party, and the director of Jackson's election campaigns.

The bank issue did not work for the National Republicans. The majority of voters across the United States viewed Jackson's stands on the bank charter and on nullification as acts of a truly democratic leader. More popular than ever, Andrew Jackson easily won four more years with 219 electoral votes to Clay's 49. He would need all his popularity for the challenges that awaited him during his second term of office.

Chapter 5

At War with the Bank ——————————

When Andrew Jackson took the oath of office for his second term as president of the United States, he was the most admired man in America. He was also the most hated. His admirers believed that he had taken the federal government away from the rich and given it back to the people. His enemies called him a dictator.

Soon after Jackson's second term began, he turned his interest once again to the Bank of the United States. The director of the bank, Nicholas Biddle, had been a leading supporter of Henry Clay. Now that Clay had lost the election, Biddle announced new bank policies, making it more difficult to borrow money. The new policies would threaten Jackson's strongest supporters—small merchants and farmers—and would slow down the government's sale of lands on the frontier to settlers.

Nicholas Biddle, director of the Bank of the United States, was one of Jackson's most powerful enemies. He prompted Jackson's determination to destroy the bank.

Jackson saw the new policies as a direct threat to his government. He decided to strike a death blow to the hated bank. He instructed his secretary of the treasury, William Duane, to remove all government deposits from the Bank of the United States and to deposit them instead in selected state banks. Duane believed that the order was wrongheaded and dangerous. He refused to carry it out. Jackson promptly fired him and named Roger Taney as the new treasury secretary, knowing that Taney would support him. By late 1833, the Bank of the United States was weakening, as government funds were withdrawn.

In order to stay in business, the bank's directors fought back. The bank demanded immediate repayment of loans it had made to smaller banks and to businesses. With shrinking funds, it stopped making new loans. These last-minute moves didn't work, however. The Bank of the United States was failing, and before its charter ran out in 1836, it had gone out of business.

This cartoon shows Jackson destroying the Bank of the United States as Biddle, Clay, and others are driven away. Biddle has the ears and the feet of a donkey or a devil.

In the meantime, selected banks across the country received huge deposits of funds from the federal government. They had been handpicked by the Jackson government, and many were run by Jackson supporters. Jackson's opponents called them Jackson's "pet banks." These pet banks saw a great opportunity. They had plenty of money to lend, and if they ran short, they printed more bills. (In Jackson's time, the government did not print paper money—each bank could print its own.)

Small borrowers were happy to be able to take out loans to buy land or expand their businesses. At the same time, the uncontrolled increase in paper money began to cause problems. The pet banks were supposed to have enough gold and silver on hand to redeem all their paper bills when customers asked. When it became clear that they didn't have the gold and silver, the value of the paper money began to decrease. Goods that cost one paper dollar soon cost two. People who had been saving money saw its value go down every day. In the old days, the Bank of the United States helped control the supply of paper money. Now that it was out of business, Jackson's advisers saw that they must find some other way to control the currency.

Finally, in 1836, Jackson issued an order known as the Specie Circular. It said that the federal government would no longer accept paper money from those who owed it money. All payments were to be made in *specie*—gold or silver. Thousands of frontier settlers who had bought their land from the government now had to make their payments in gold or silver coins. They rushed to the banks, demanding to receive coins for their paper bills. The banks soon ran out of gold and silver and were not able to redeem the paper. The value of paper bills fell lower and lower. Individuals and businesses struggled to pay their debts and people hoping to borrow money were turned down. With the money supply drying up, unemployment rose and many of the people Jackson wanted to help were broke and hungry.

The Whigs

The nation's financial problems gave Jackson's enemies an opportunity to attack him with new strength. The National Republicans—the party of John Quincy Adams and Henry Clay—joined with others opposed to Jackson's policies and formed the Whig Party in 1834. They took their name from the Whig party in Britain, which had fought the tyrannical power of the English monarchy for 150 years. The American Whigs formed to fight the tyranny of Andrew Jackson, who appeared in political cartoons of the time with royal robes and the title "King Andrew the First."

BORN TO COMMAND

OF VETO MEMORY

HAD I BEEN CONSULTED

KING ANDREW the FIRST

This cartoon, published by the Whigs, shows Jackson as "King Andrew the First." He is trampling on the U.S. Constitution and on the charter of the Bank of the United States.

The powerful men in Congress were especially angry because Jackson refused to work with them, vetoed their legislation, and appealed over their heads to the people of the country. In the spring of 1834, Henry Clay called for the U.S. Senate to pass a resolution censuring (condemning) the president for overstepping the bounds of his office. The Senate passed the resolution. The House of Representatives, which had a majority of Jackson supporters, took no action. Three years later, just before Jackson left the White House, the Senate expunged (erased) its vote of censure.

Indian Removal

From the beginning of his presidency, Jackson owed some of his popularity to his long record as an enemy of Native Americans. Voters remembered not only his victory over the British at New Orleans, but also his victory over the Creek people at Horseshoe Bend and his pursuit of the Seminole raiders into Florida.

Jackson believed that Native Americans should be removed from lands settlers wanted, especially in the Old Southwest (present-day Tennessee, Alabama, Mississippi, and Louisiana). To Jackson and to most of the residents of the region, the Cherokee, Chickasaw, Choctaw, Creek, and Seminole were simply in the way of whites, who needed more land for farms and towns. Fear and suspicion of Native Americans ran deep. Jackson doubted that Native

Americans and settlers would ever be able to coexist in peace. He believed that removing them to the west, beyond the Mississippi River, was the only solution. Early in his first term, he pushed through Congress the Indian Removal Act of 1830. This legislation appropriated money to pay Native Americans small sums for their huge territories and to arrange for their move to an Indian territory west of the Mississippi.

Many people in the country were troubled by the cruel treatment Native Americans had received from local authorities and the U.S. government. Yet even many of these people agreed to the plan for Indian removal. Jackson himself tried to show the positive side of the policy. "Say to [the Indians]," he wrote to one Indian agent, "where they now are, they and my white children are too near to each other to live in harmony and peace. . . . Beyond the great river Missippi [*sic*] . . . , their father has provided a country, large enough for them all, and he advises them to remove to it. There, their white brethren will not trouble them . . . and they can live upon it, they and all their children as long as grass grows or water runs in peace and plenty. It will be theirs forever."

Some Indians fought the law in the courts. In one famous case, the U.S. Supreme Court ruled in their favor. Jackson and state officials ignored the Supreme Court ruling, however, and the tribe lost its lands anyway. The Seminole

The chief justice of the Supreme Court, John Marshall, ruled in favor of Cherokee land claims in Georgia in 1831. President Jackson did not enforce the court's decision, however, and the Cherokee lost their land anyway.

in Florida waged war against the U.S. Army when it tried to remove them. Finally, starting during Jackson's second term and continuing for several years after he left office, the Indians of the Old Southwest were stripped of their lands and forced to move to the west at gunpoint.

The Indian removal was a dark chapter in American history. Native Americans were forced to sell their lands for pennies and then herded like cattle to the western lands. Some 16,000 Cherokee men, women, and children were sent 800 miles (1,300 km) along what became known as the "Trail of Tears." One of every four perished along the way from cold, starvation, or disease. Their new homes often turned out to be barren wastelands, and many Indians later rebelled, leading to further bloodshed in the years to come.

Jackson's unbending policy on Native Americans received widespread support in his day. He had some sympathy for Native Americans and believed that in some way he was protecting them. He never took them seriously, however, seeming to think of them as children in need of stern discipline. Like African American slaves, Native Americans were considered less important—and perhaps less human—than white settlers descended from European ancestors. However popular Indian removal was in the 1830s, it appears today as a tragic episode in American history and a blemish on Jackson's record.

Assassin!

On January 30, 1835, while he was attending the funeral of a U.S. congressman, Jackson stepped onto the east porch of the Capitol. As he was about to reenter the building, a bearded young man stepped forward, drew a small pistol, aimed it directly at Jackson's chest, and pulled the trigger. The shot rang out. Jackson lunged toward his attacker, his walking stick raised to strike. The young man aimed a second gun and pulled the trigger. A second explosion rang out. Jackson struck again at the attacker, and an onlooker wrestled the gunman to the ground. On both shots, the firing caps went off, but the main charge of gunpowder had failed to ignite. Fortunately, Jackson was unhurt.

It turned out that the attacker was an unemployed, mentally ill housepainter named Richard Lawrence. He believed that he was the heir to the British throne and that Jackson was keeping him from his proper place as king of England. Lawrence was tried for the attack but found not guilty because of insanity and sent to an asylum.

This was the first time an assassin attempted to kill a U.S. president. In the future there would be other attempts. Four later U.S. presidents would be killed by assassins.

☆ ☆ ☆

Foreign Policy

Jackson's eight years as president were concerned mostly with *domestic affairs*, events and actions within the United States. In *foreign affairs*, there were no wars or other major crises. Still, Jackson worked to maintain the stature of the United

States among the nations of the world. He established diplomatic relations for the first time with Siam (present-day Thailand) and other Asian countries, and signed commercial treaties with others, promoting American trade.

Jackson dealt sternly with France. The French had refused for years to pay reparations to American shipowners for damages caused by the French navy during the Napoleonic Wars more than twenty years earlier. When further diplomacy failed, Jackson warned that if payment was not made, the American people would seize French property. In 1836, France agreed to make the payments.

Texas

The most important foreign business during Jackson's presidency concerned Mexico and the status of Texas, then a Mexican territory. The region had been a possession of Spain, then became part of Mexico, which declared its independence in 1821. The region was very thinly settled until settlers from the American south began to move into the territory in the 1830s.

Jackson believed it would be a good idea to *annex* Texas (make it part of the United States). It would provide a buffer between Mexico and the United States. During his first term in office, he tried to buy the region, but the Mexican government refused his offer. In 1836, during Jackson's second term, the American settlers in Texas revolted against the Mexican government and declared their independence. Mexico sent troops to reclaim the territory, but they were defeated. Soon afterward, Texans requested the U.S. government to annex Texas as a territory.

This presented Jackson with a difficult choice. He favored annexing the territory, and the first president of Texas, Sam Houston, was an old friend from Tennessee. On the other hand, there were two strong reasons *not* to annex Texas. First, it was clear that American annexation would lead to a war with Mexico, which still claimed the territory. Second, there was strong opposition to annexing Texas in the United States, especially among northerners, who opposed slavery. They could see that Texas would one day become a new slave state.

Sam Houston

Born in Virginia in 1793, Sam Houston served with Andrew Jackson during the Creek War in 1814. He was later Jackson's aide, living for a time at The Hermitage. In 1823, Houston was elected to Congress as a representative from Tennessee and later served as the state's governor. He resigned as governor in 1829 and moved to Texas in 1832. In Texas, he commanded the army that defeated the Mexicans at the Battle of San Jacinto, April 21, 1836, winning Texas independence. He was elected president of Texas the same year. After Texas became a state, Houston was elected to the U.S. Senate for two terms. In 1859, he was elected governor of Texas. He died in 1863.

Jackson never did move to annex Texas. On his last day in office, however, he gave diplomatic recognition to the Republic of Texas as a legitimate government.

The End of the Presidency

As his second term neared its end, Jackson was more than ready to leave the White House. At the age of 69, he was a sick man, suffering from a variety of ailments. Following the practice of all earlier presidents, he announced his plan to retire.

Jackson let the new Democratic party know that he favored Martin Van Buren to be their nominee for the presidency in 1836. Van Buren had been one of Jackson's closest advisers and most loyal supporters from the beginning of his presidency. He served first as secretary of state, and he was elected in 1832 as Jackson's vice president. In 1836, riding the continuing wave of Jackson's popularity, Van Buren was elected the eighth president of the United States.

In his farewell speech on the day of Van Buren's inauguration, Jackson said he was happy to have presided over the nation at a time when special privilege no longer ruled. He noted that he was near the end of his own life. "I thank God," he said, "that my life has been spent in a land of liberty and that He has given me a heart to love my country with the affection of a son."

Andrew Jackson late in his presidency. Although often ill and in pain, he still stood tall.

When Van Buren was sworn in, an estimated 20,000 people stood silent, paying homage to the departing Jackson. "It was the stillness and silence of reverence and affection," said one observer, "and there was no room for mistake as to whom this mute and impressive homage was rendered. For once, the rising was eclipsed by the setting sun."

Chapter 6

Retirement

In March 1837, Andrew Jackson left Washington, D.C., and returned to The Hermitage. At almost every stop he made in the long journey, he was greeted by cheering crowds who wanted to see the man so many considered the protector of the people.

Jackson was deeply moved by the love and respect he was shown on this journey. "This is truly the patriot's reward, and a source of great gratification to me, and it will be solace to the grave," the ex-president wrote to Martin Van Buren.

Once at home, the ex-president found little rest. During his time in Washington, Old Hickory had put his adopted son, Andrew Jackson Jr., in charge of his business affairs. Andrew Jr. had no head for business. He ran up bills he could not pay. He borrowed money for friends which they never paid back. Because The Hermitage and the

The Hermitage, Jackson's home outside of Nashville, where he lived in retirement. Like many fine southern mansions, it was built in the style called Greek Revival, featuring stately columns along the front.

Jacksons' other interests were a family business, Andrew Jackson was duty-bound to help pay his stepson's debts. It would take most of his remaining years to free himself from the weight of those debts.

Jackson was also saddened to see that the nation was fast sinking into a severe financial depression. Not long after he returned to Tennessee, banks in many parts of the country began to fail. Farmers could not sell their crops, and many in cities were thrown out of work. In several large cities, hungry mobs rioted.

The depression was partly caused by economic troubles in Europe, but many (especially the Whigs) blamed the suffering on Jackson's war against the Bank of the United States. Now they clamored for President Van Buren to do something to ease the suf-

President Martin Van Buren's term was darkened by the severe Panic of 1837, which was partly caused by Jackson's economic policies.

fering. When he did not act quickly enough, they began blaming him.

By 1840, the new Democratic party had lost much of its popularity. The Whigs took advantage of the situation, persuading voters that it was time for a change. They nominated William Henry Harrison to run against Van Buren. Like

Jackson, Harrison was a military hero famous for victories in the Indian wars and the War of 1812. After a campaign appealing to the common people, the Whigs and Harrison defeated Van Buren and sent him into retirement.

Since Van Buren was his chosen successor, Jackson saw the defeat as a personal affront. The sadness, however, did not last long. Within a month of his inauguration, Harrison died of pneumonia. His vice president, John Tyler, took his place as president. Tyler, a former Democrat who had recently become a Whig, proved to favor many Democratic policies. When he vetoed a bill for a new Bank of the United States, the Whigs expelled him from their party. On another topic—Texas—Tyler also stood with Jackson. He favored the annexation of the Lone Star Republic as a territory.

Throughout his retirement, Jackson stayed politically active. He wrote many letters to other politicians and frequently entertained government leaders at his plantation. As the presidential election of 1844 approached, Jackson first favored his old friend Van Buren. The issue of Texas, however, finally divided these two old partners. Van Buren still opposed annexing Texas, but Jackson thought that the time for annexation had come. Before the Democratic convention, he shifted his support to James K. Polk, an old friend and supporter from Tennessee. In the campaign, Polk received the nickname "Young Hickory" to

Jackson remained a powerful political force in retirement. In 1844, he threw his support behind his fellow Tennessean James K. Polk for president, and Polk was elected.

emphasize his connection with Jackson. Running on a platform of annexing Texas, Polk defeated Whig candidate Henry Clay. Jackson must have smiled when he heard the news.

Death

The Hero of New Orleans had little to smile about as 1844 ended and 1845 began. His health continued to decline. He had frequent lung infections and still suffered from severe headaches and diarrhea.

A portrait of Jackson painted in 1845, near the end of his life, shows a man who looks almost ghostly, with a shock of white hair like a halo over a skeletal face. Still, Jackson kept busy with his letter-writing and visitors. When he felt up to it, he rode his horse around his plantation. Late in the day, when he was not bedridden, he would walk slowly, leaning on his cane, to where his wife, Rachel, lay buried.

By early June 1845, Jackson was feeble, in pain, and unable to get up from bed. On Sunday, June 8, a doctor visited. As soon as he saw Jackson, he knew he was dying. During the morning of that day, the ex-president drifted in and out of consciousness. At one point, when he heard his slaves weeping, he asked them not to grieve.

"My dear children, and friends, and servants," he said, "I hope and trust to meet you all in heaven, both white and black."

That afternoon, Jackson spoke to family and friends who had gathered around his bed. He talked of his impending death. At that, all in the room began weeping.

"Have I alarmed you?" Jackson asked. "Oh, do not cry. Be good children, and we will all meet in heaven."

At six o'clock in the evening, Andrew Jackson died quietly. Two days later, on June 10, 1845, he was buried in a grave by the side of his beloved wife.

Jackson's Legacy

Andrew Jackson was a true hero to most Americans in his own time. He was the perfect model of the American self-made man, born into poor circumstances, an orphan at an early age, who went on to become a successful lawyer and farmer, and a military hero. He ran for president as an outsider, yet succeeded in becoming the most powerful president the United States had yet seen.

This cartoon shows Jackson, dressed in military uniform, towering over many opponents and critics, who are shown as barking dogs.

Jackson brought a new sense of democracy to the government, appointing people to high government positions who had no family or college connections and who came from every section of the country. In the great crisis of his presidency, nullification, he spoke powerfully in favor of the Union and the rights of the federal government. At the same time, however, he resisted greater federal spending and supported strong, active states.

His greatest accomplishment was to create a more powerful presidency. He claimed that the president, as the one official elected by all the people of the United States, represents the people against the regional and special interests of members of Congress. Using his powerful personality and his conviction of being in the right, he convinced a majority of voters that he did indeed represent their wishes.

Some of Jackson's other accomplishments are troubling to modern historians. He succeeded in killing the hated Bank of the United States. His war against the bank made him a popular hero fighting for small farmers and tradesmen against wealthy bankers and merchants. Yet today, this accomplishment is controversial. Was the death of the bank a step forward or a step in the wrong direction? After Jackson left office the country went through a severe depression that was partly caused by his policies.

Jackson's campaign against Native Americans and his support of slavery in the south also added to his popularity. His beliefs about Native Americans and

African Americans and his actions against them seem cruel and unjust to many today.

Jackson was also a difficult personality. He could be loving and caring to his wife and family, but he could be impulsive and violent and was cruel and vindictive to his enemies. He rarely doubted that his own judgment of people and issues was right. Some say his main aim was not to serve the common people but to gain power and approval.

Even people who condemn many of Jackson's policies agree that he was one of most powerful and influential presidents in American history. He brought new energy to the national government. He oversaw the creation of a political party that sought to represent all the people, rather than the rich and the influential. He helped redefine the powers of the presidency. In addition, he expressed new confidence in the country and its future. All of this has caused scholars to give his name to the era he lived in—the "Age of Jackson." No other president has been recognized in this way.

Fast Facts Andrew Jackson

Birth:	March 15, 1767
Birthplace:	The Waxhaws, South Carolina
Parents:	Andrew Jackson and Elizabeth Hutchinson Jackson
Brothers:	Hugh Jackson (1763 or 1764–1780)
	Robert Jackson (1765 or 1766–1781)
Education:	Local schools
Occupations:	Lawyer, judge, soldier
Marriage:	To Rachel Donelson Robards, 1791, Natchez, Mississippi; remarried 1794, Nashville, Tennessee
Children:	Andrew Jackson Jr. (Rachel Jackson's nephew), adopted 1809; several foster children
Political Party:	Democratic-Republican; Democratic
Public Offices:	1796 Member, U.S. House of Representatives from Tennessee
	1797 U.S. Senator from Tennessee
	1798–1804 Judge, Tennessee Superior Court
	1821 Governor, Florida Territory
	1823–1825 U.S. Senator from Tennessee
	1829–1837 Seventh President of the United States
His Vice Presidents:	1829–1832 John C. Calhoun
	1833–1837 Martin Van Buren
Major Actions as President:	1830 Signed Indian Removal Act
	1831 Accepted cabinet resignations resulting from the "Petticoat War"
	1832 Vetoed bill rechartering Bank of the United States
	1833 Compromise ended nullification crisis
	1837 Recognized government of the Republic of Texas
Firsts:	President not from Massachusetts or Virginia
	President born in a log cabin
	President to exercise a veto on non-Constitutional grounds
	President to face an assassination attempt
	President to be censured by the U.S. Senate
Death:	June 8, 1845
Age at Death:	78 years
Burial Place:	The Hermitage, near Nashville, Tennessee

Fast Facts

Rachel Donelson Robards Jackson

Birth:	1767
Birthplace:	Virginia
Parents:	John Donelson and Rachel Stockley Donelson
Brother & Sisters:	7 brothers; 3 sisters
Education:	Taught at home
Marriages:	To Lewis Robards, 1784 or 1785, Virginia (divorced); To Andrew Jackson, 1791, Natchez, Mississippi; remarried, 1794, Nashville, Tennessee
Children:	[*see* Andrew Jackson at left]
Death:	December 22, 1828
Age at Death:	61 years
Burial Place:	The Hermitage, outside Nashville, Tennessee

Timeline

1767	1780–81	1784	1787	1788
Andrew Jackson born March 15, in the Waxhaws region, near the South Carolina-North Carolina border, weeks after the death of his father	Older brother Hugh dies; Andrew serves in the American Revolution, is captured by the British and wounded by an officer; contracts smallpox; brother Robert and mother die	Moves to Salisbury, North Carolina; studies law	Licensed as an attorney on September 26	Moves to Nashville, Tennessee, serves as public prosecutor

1802	1804	1806	1813	1814
Elected major general of the Tennessee militia; fights duel with John Sevier	Resigns as judge; purchases Hermitage property	Duels with Charles Dickinson; Jackson is badly wounded, but kills Dickinson	Commissioned in U.S. Army for War of 1812; leads army south to Natchez and back to Nashville; wounded in gun battle in Nashville; leads army against Creek Indians	Defeats Creek Indians at Horseshoe Bend, in present-day Alabama

1825	1828	1830	1831	1832
House of Representatives elects John Quincy Adams president; Jackson charges Adams and Henry Clay stole election; resigns from Senate	Elected the seventh president of the U.S. (November); Rachel Jackson dies (December 22); Jackson inaugurated in March 1829	Signs Indian Removal Act	Accepts resignations of cabinet members after the "Petticoat War"	Vetoes bill to recharter Bank of the United States; reelected president, defeating Henry Clay

1791	1794	1796	1797	1798
Marries Rachel Donelson Robards	Jackson and Rachel remarry after discovering her divorce was not final until 1793	Serves as delegate to Tennessee Constitutional Convention; elected first U.S. congressman from Tennessee	Elected to U.S. Senate	Resigns from Senate; elected a judge of the Tennessee superior court

1815	1818	1821	1823	1824
Defeats British at Battle of New Orleans	Pursues Seminole Indians into Spanish territory of Florida; captures Spanish forts	Serves as governor of new U.S. Florida Territory	Elected to U.S. Senate	Wins most popular and electoral votes in presidential election, but not the required majority

1833	1833	1836	1837	1845
Threatens military force against South Carolina in nullification crisis; signs compromise tariff bill, ending the crisis	Withdraws federal funds from the Bank of the United States, leading to its collapse	Announces his retirement, supports Vice President Van Buren for president; Van Buren elected	Gives diplomatic recognition to Republic of Texas; retires to The Hermitage	Jackson dies June 8; he is buried next to Rachel in the garden of The Hermitage

Glossary

abolitionist: in U.S. history, a supporter of ending (abolishing) slavery in all states and territories

annex: the action of a country making a new region part of its territory

assassinate: to kill a government leader

bigamy: being married to two people at one time

censure: to condemn the actions of a political or military leader officially

charter: a license granted by a government permitting a company to operate

conspiracy: a secret plot between two or more people to commit a crime

domestic affairs: government business involving actions within its borders; *see also* **foreign affairs**

duel: a formal contest (often with swords or handguns) between two gentlemen to avenge an insult

foreign affairs: government business involving relations with other countries and actions outside its borders; *see also* **domestic affairs**

nullify: in U.S. history, the refusal of a state to obey or enforce a law passed by the federal government because the state considers the law unconstitutional

secede: in U.S. history, an action by a state to leave the government of the United States

specie: coins or precious metal used as payment of a debt instead of paper money

tariff: a tax on goods imported into a country

veto: in U.S. government, a president's refusal to sign a bill passed by Congress into law; Congress may **override** a veto by passing the bill by two-thirds majorities in the House and Senate.

Further Reading

Behrman, Carol. *Andrew Jackson*. Minneapolis: Lerner, 2002.

Judson, Karen. *Andrew Jackson*. Springfield, NJ: Enslow, 1997.

Meltzer, Milton. *Andrew Jackson and His America*. New York: Franklin Watts, 1993.

Tallant, Robert. *Pirate Lafitte and the Battle of New Orleans*. Gretna, LA: Pelican, 1992.

Viola, Herman. *Andrew Jackson*. Broomall, PA: Chelsea House, 1987.

Warrick, Karen. *The War of 1812: We Have Met the Enemy and They Are Ours*. Springfield, NJ: Enslow, 2002.

MORE ADVANCED READING

Burstein, Andrew. *The Passions of Andrew Jackson*. New York: Knopf, 2003.

Remini, Robert. *Andrew Jackson and His Indian Wars*. New York: Viking Penguin, 2001.

——. *The Battle of New Orleans: Andrew Jackson and America's First Military Victory*. New York: Viking Penguin, 1999.

——. *The Life of Andrew Jackson*. New York: Harper-Collins, 1988.

Places to Visit

★ ★ ★ ★ ★

The Hermitage

4580 Rachel's Lane

Nashville, TN 37076-1344

(615) 889-2941

www.thehermitage.com

Andrew Jackson's plantation and home is open to tours. Guides dressed in costumes from Jackson's time show the restored mansion, tell stories of Jackson and his family, and point out his belongings, including a sword. The Hermitage, located about 12 miles east of downtown Nashville, Tennessee, is accessible from Interstate 40, exit 221 (The Hermitage exit). Nashville historical sites also include several early homes and a replica of Fort Nashboro, the enclosed village that grew to be the town of Nashville.

Chalmette Battlefield

8606 West St. Bernard Highway

Chalmette, LA 70043-4204

(504) 281-0510

www.nps.gov/jela/Chalmette%20Battlefield.htm

The battlefield where Jackson and his troops defeated the British in the Battle of New Orleans on January 8, 1815. Visitors can walk the ramparts behind which Jackson's men stood during the battle and see cannon from the era.

Horseshoe Bend Battlefield

11288 Horseshoe Bend Road

Daviston, AL 36256-9751

(256) 234-7111

The site of Jackson's victory over the Creek during the War of 1812.

Online Sites of Interest

★ **Internet Public Library, Presidents of the United States (IPL-POTUS)**

http://ipl.si.umich.edu/div/potus/ajackson.html

Provides a brief biography of Jackson and many useful links to other Internet sites.

★ **American Presidents**

http://www.americanpresidents.org/

Provides useful biographies of each president based on materials gathered for a public television series.

★ **The White House**

http://www.whitehouse.gov/history/presidents/aj7.html

Biography and interesting facts about Andrew Jackson. The site also provides additional information on the historic residence, first ladies, and topics of current interest.

★ **Rachel Jackson**

http://www.wnpt.net/rachel/

A biography of Rachel Jackson, along with information about her family and the early history of Nashville, Tennessee.

★ **The Battle of Horseshoe Bend**

http://www.cr.nps.gov/nr/twhp/wwwlps/lessons/54horseshoe/54horseshoe.htm

Examines Jackson's army, the Creek peoples he defeated, and the continuing conflict between the United States and Native Americans.

★ **The Battle of New Orleans**

http://lsm.crt.state.la.us/cabildo/cab6.htm

Provides a summary of the battle and informative art and photographs.

★ **Indian Removal**

http://www.ourdocuments.gov/content.php?page=document&doc=25

Jackson's speech to Congress explaining and defending his policy of removing Native Americans to reservations west of the Mississippi River.

Table of Presidents

	1. George Washington	**2. John Adams**	**3. Thomas Jefferson**	**4. James Madison**
Took office	Apr 30 1789	Mar 4 1797	Mar 4 1801	Mar 4 1809
Left office	Mar 3 1797	Mar 3 1801	Mar 3 1809	Mar 3 1817
Birthplace	Westmoreland Co, VA	Braintree, MA	Shadwell, VA	Port Conway, VA
Birth date	Feb 22 1732	Oct 20 1735	Apr 13 1743	Mar 16 1751
Death date	Dec 14 1799	July 4 1826	July 4 1826	June 28 1836

   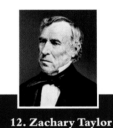

	9. William H. Harrison	**10. John Tyler**	**11. James K. Polk**	**12. Zachary Taylor**
Took office	Mar 4 1841	Apr 6 1841	Mar 4 1845	Mar 5 1849
Left office	**Apr 4 1841•**	Mar 3 1845	Mar 3 1849	**July 9 1850•**
Birthplace	Berkeley, VA	Greenway, VA	Mecklenburg Co, NC	Barboursville, VA
Birth date	Feb 9 1773	Mar 29 1790	Nov 2 1795	Nov 24 1784
Death date	Apr 4 1841	Jan 18 1862	June 15 1849	July 9 1850

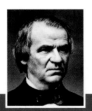   

	17. Andrew Johnson	**18. Ulysses S. Grant**	**19. Rutherford B. Hayes**	**20. James A. Garfield**
Took office	Apr 15 1865	Mar 4 1869	Mar 4 1877	Mar 4 1881
Left office	Mar 3 1869	Mar 3 1877	Mar 3 1881	**Sept 19 1881•**
Birthplace	Raleigh, NC	Point Pleasant, OH	Delaware, OH	Orange, OH
Birth date	Dec 29 1808	Apr 27 1822	Oct 4 1822	Nov 19 1831
Death date	July 31 1875	July 23 1885	Jan 17 1893	Sept 19 1881

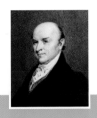

5. James Monroe	6. John Quincy Adams	7. Andrew Jackson	8. Martin Van Buren
Mar 4 1817	Mar 4 1825	Mar 4 1829	Mar 4 1837
Mar 3 1825	Mar 3 1829	Mar 3 1837	Mar 3 1841
Westmoreland Co, VA	Braintree, MA	The Waxhaws, SC	Kinderhook, NY
Apr 28 1758	July 11 1767	Mar 15 1767	Dec 5 1782
July 4 1831	Feb 23 1848	June 8 1845	July 24 1862

13. Millard Fillmore	14. Franklin Pierce	15. James Buchanan	16. Abraham Lincoln
July 9 1850	Mar 4 1853	Mar 4 1857	Mar 4 1861
Mar 3 1853	Mar 3 1857	Mar 3 1861	**Apr 15 1865•**
Locke Township, NY	Hillsborough, NH	Cove Gap, PA	Hardin Co, KY
Jan 7 1800	Nov 23 1804	Apr 23 1791	Feb 12 1809
Mar 8 1874	Oct 8 1869	June 1 1868	Apr 15 1865

21. Chester A. Arthur	22. Grover Cleveland	23. Benjamin Harrison	24. Grover Cleveland
Sept 19 1881	Mar 4 1885	Mar 4 1889	Mar 4 1893
Mar 3 1885	Mar 3 1889	Mar 3 1893	Mar 3 1897
Fairfield, VT	Caldwell, NJ	North Bend, OH	Caldwell, NJ
Oct 5 1830	Mar 18 1837	Aug 20 1833	Mar 18 1837
Nov 18 1886	June 24 1908	Mar 13 1901	June 24 1908

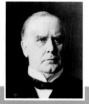   

	25. William McKinley	**26. Theodore Roosevelt**	**27. William H. Taft**	**28. Woodrow Wilson**
Took office	Mar 4 1897	Sept 14 1901	Mar 4 1909	Mar 4 1913
Left office	**Sept 14 1901•**	Mar 3 1909	Mar 3 1913	Mar 3 1921
Birthplace	Niles, OH	New York, NY	Cincinnati, OH	Staunton, VA
Birth date	Jan 29 1843	Oct 27 1858	Sept 15 1857	Dec 28 1856
Death date	Sept 14 1901	Jan 6 1919	Mar 8 1930	Feb 3 1924

	33. Harry S. Truman	**34. Dwight D. Eisenhower**	**35. John F. Kennedy**	**36. Lyndon B. Johnson**
Took office	Apr 12 1945	Jan 20 1953	Jan 20 1961	Nov 22 1963
Left office	Jan 20 1953	Jan 20 1961	**Nov 22 1963•**	Jan 20 1969
Birthplace	Lamar, MO	Denison, TX	Brookline, MA	Johnson City, TX
Birth date	May 8 1884	Oct 14 1890	May 29 1917	Aug 27 1908
Death date	Dec 26 1972	Mar 28 1969	Nov 22 1963	Jan 22 1973

	41. George Bush	**42. Bill Clinton**	**43. George W. Bush**	
Took office	Jan 20 1989	Jan 20 1993	Jan 20 2001	
Left office	Jan 20 1993	Jan 20 2001	—	
Birthplace	Milton, MA	Hope, AR	New Haven, CT	
Birth date	June 12 1924	Aug 19 1946	July 6 1946	
Death date	—	—	—	

29. Warren G. Harding	**30. Calvin Coolidge**	**31. Herbert Hoover**	**32. Franklin D. Roosevelt**
Mar 4 1921	Aug 2 1923	Mar 4 1929	Mar 4 1933
Aug 2 1923•	Mar 3 1929	Mar 3 1933	**Apr 12 1945•**
Blooming Grove, OH	Plymouth, VT	West Branch, IA	Hyde Park, NY
Nov 21 1865	July 4 1872	Aug 10 1874	Jan 30 1882
Aug 2 1923	Jan 5 1933	Oct 20 1964	Apr 12 1945

37. Richard M. Nixon	**38. Gerald R. Ford**	**39. Jimmy Carter**	**40. Ronald Reagan**
Jan 20 1969	Aug 9 1974	Jan 20 1977	Jan 20 1981
Aug 9 1974★	Jan 20 1977	Jan 20 1981	Jan 20 1989
Yorba Linda, CA	Omaha, NE	Plains, GA	Tampico, IL
Jan 9 1913	July 14 1913	Oct 1 1924	Feb 11 1911
Apr 22 1994	—	—	—

• Indicates the president died while in office.

★ Richard Nixon resigned before his term expired.

Index

★ ★ ★ ★ ★

About the Author

Kieran Doherty is the award-winning author of a dozen nonfiction books for young readers. A career journalist and magazine writer before turning his attention to writing for young readers, he particularly enjoys writing about heroic figures from American history. Doherty lives in Lake Worth, Florida, with his wife.